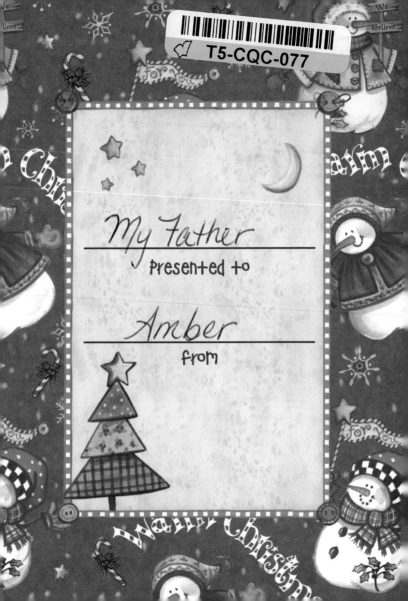

T5-CQC-077

My Father

presented to

Amber

from

# Joy Notes at Christmas

WARM WISHES

JUST FOR YOU, DAD!

WELCOME WINTER

WINTER WELCOME WINTER

I love Christmas

WARM WISHES

COUNTRYMAN

Copyright of illustrations © 2001 by Debra Jordan Bryan
Published by J. Countryman
A division of Thomas Nelson, Inc.,
Nashville, Tennessee 37214

Project Editor—Terri Gibbs

Designed by Left Coast Design, Portland, Oregon

ISBN: 0-8499-9540-X

www.jcountryman.com

Printed in China

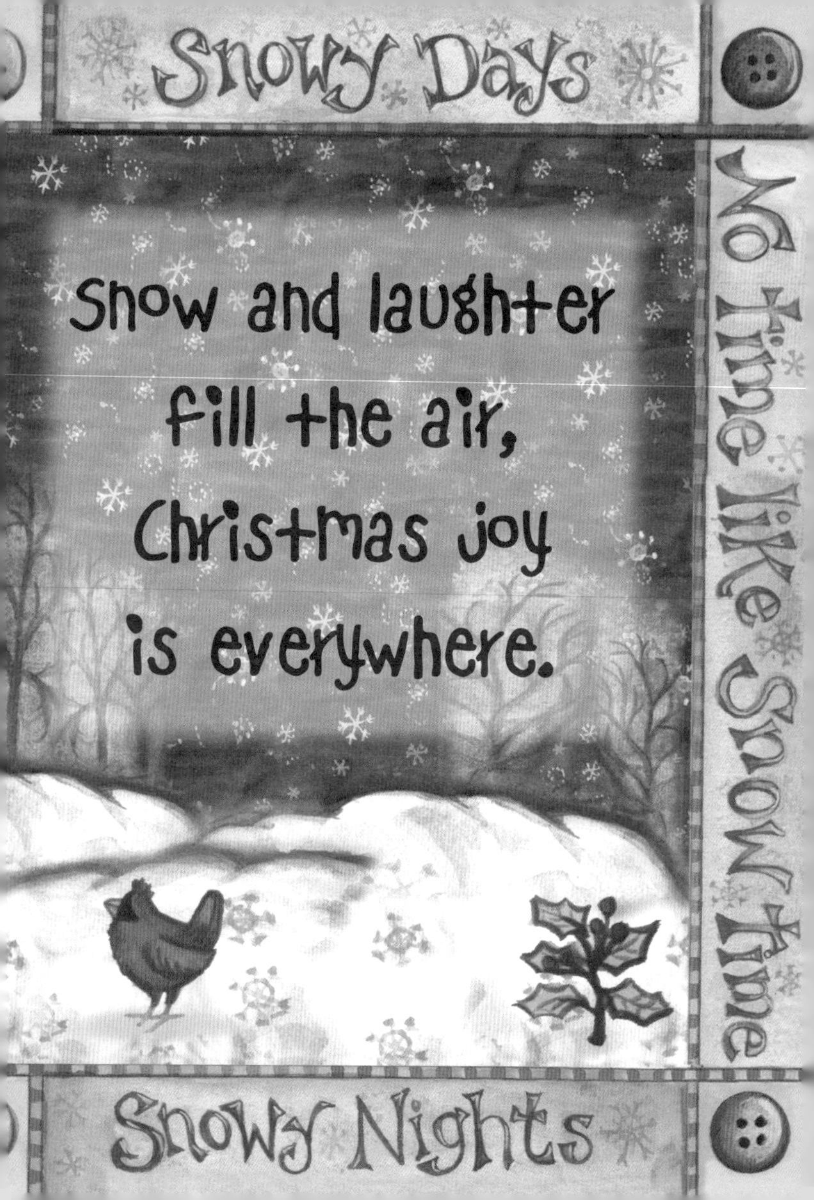

Snowy Days
No Time like Snow Time
Snowy Nights

Snow and laughter
fill the air,
Christmas joy
is everywhere.

You are a
Special Part
of our Family

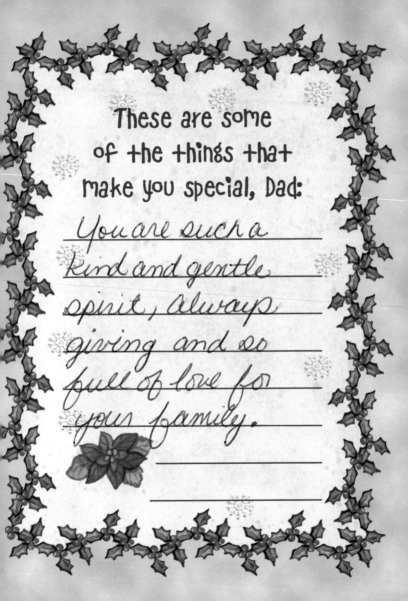

These are some
of the things that
make you special, Dad:

_You are such a_

_kind and gentle_

_spirit, always_

_giving and so_

_full of love for_

_your family._

perfect gift

Every good and

is from above.

I love Christmas

James 1:17

You are
God's gift
to me.

Hearts go home at Christmas...

Mittens 4 SALE

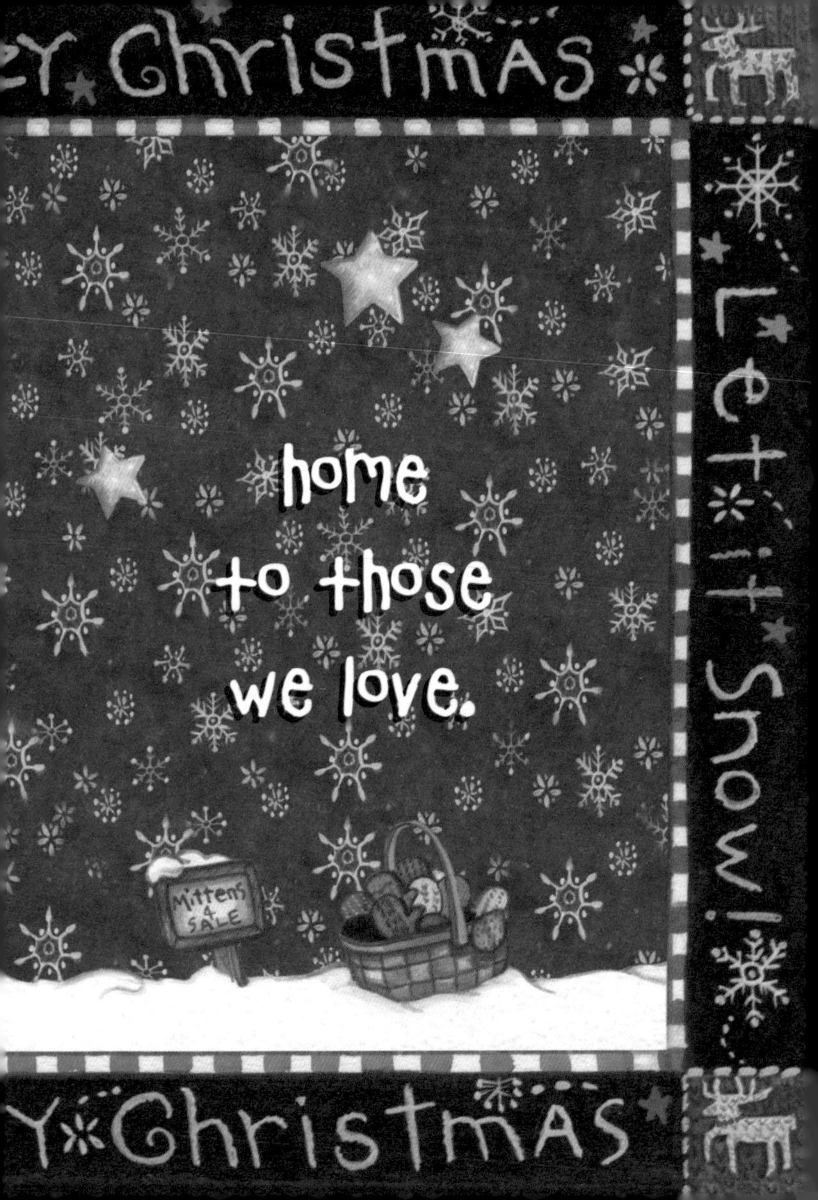


home
to those
we love.

A gift can
be large,
A gift can
be small,
but a gift wrapped
in love is the
best gift of all.

We believe in Christmas

We believe in Christmas

If I could give you
any gift in the world
I'd give you the
gift of...

Peace within
yourself and with
the Lord and good
health that
will keep you
here with those
who love you
dearly.

Let's celebrate this
time of year...

when hope
and joy
and love appear.

Let heaven
and nature
and your own
heart sing!

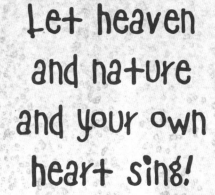

# My Christmas prayer
## for you, Dad:

Thank You Lord for giving me the best Father I could ever ask for. May your angels watch over him and bless him. In Jesus name I pray — Amen.

Let's shout
out our
welcome
to the
wonders of
the season.

Carols ring
through
crisp, cold air...
God bless us
everyone!